HERBAL
HOMEKEEPING

HERBAL HOMEKEEPING

Sandy Maine

INTERWEAVE PRESS

Herbal Homekeeping
By Sandy Maine

Cover and book design: Dean Howes
Photo Styling: Ann Sabin Swanson
Photography: Joe Coca

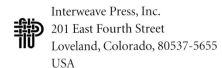
Interweave Press, Inc.
201 East Fourth Street
Loveland, Colorado, 80537-5655
USA

Printed in China by Midas

Library of Congress Cataloging-in-Publication Data

Maine, Sandy. 1957–
    Herbal homekeeping / by Sandy Maine.
        p.   cm.
    Includes index.
    ISBN 1-883010-55-1
    1. House cleaning. 2. Herbs 3. Recipes. I. Title.
TX324.M35 1999
648'.5—dc21   99-10975
                                                            CIP

First Printing: 7.5M:599:CC

DEDICATION

I wrote this book at my home at EcoVillage, a new co-housing community of 135 people near Ithaca, New York.

It was there on an old wooden bench in the herb garden behind Unit 118 that I wrote this practical and philosophical work about herbal homekeeping and the healthy simplicity it brings to life.

I dedicate this book to the residents of EcoVillage. The distant sounds of their happy voices blended with the beautiful landscape and nourished my spirit as I wrote. I'm also grateful for the lively pond that inspired me despite hours of sitting.

I hope this book will help you fulfill your vision of ecological living and bring us all another step closer to more thoughtful ways of caring for our Earth, our homes, and ourselves.

TABLE OF CONTENTS

Centuries of Scrubbing

The History of Housekeeping ◆ *Modern Times* ◆ *A Second American Revolution*
A Big Turnaround

Rhythm, Synergy, and Satisfaction

The Danish Way ◆ *Synergy* ◆ *Divvy Up the Household Chores* ◆ *Make Tasks*
Enjoyable ◆ *Secrets for Increasing Your Homekeeping Satisfaction*

Herbal Homekeeping

Twenty Bad Reasons for This Chapter ◆ *Twenty-Three Good Reasons* ◆ *Creating a*
Gentle Cleaning Cupboard ◆ *Other Useful Equipment*

Recipes for General Cleaning

Eucalyptus, Lavender, and Tea Tree Spray Cleaner ◆ *Carnauba and Lavender*
Furniture Wax ◆ *Lavender-Ginger Suds Upholstery Cleaner and Rug*
Shampoo ◆ *Lemon-Mint Window Wash* ◆ *Lemon Metal Cleaner*

Kitchen and Bath

Key Lime Dish Detergent Powder ◆ *Eucalyptus-Mint All-Purpose Disinfecting*
Soft Soap for Kitchen and Bath ◆ *Grapefruit Abrasive Cleanser* ◆ *Russian*
Dishwashing Disk ◆ *Spritz–and–Spray Toilet Bowl Cleaner* ◆ *Blue Angel Swirl*
Toilet Bowl Cleaner

Introduction

The next time you're dashing down the cleaning-products aisle of your local supermarket, searching for your favorite items, STOP!

Look at how many cleaning products are available, and the shelf-feet of space they take. I see an amazing irony on those shelves: All those cleaning products, offered to make your homekeeping duties easier, actually *complicate* life. They also waste valuable natural resources, time, money, and space. They create certain kinds of stress, too—and nobody needs that.

Space. How many plastic bottles and containers can you fit under your kitchen sink? Advertisers would have us believe that we need a different product for each surface in the home and for every messy possibility: dust, grease, mud, pet tracks, clothing stains.

Toxicity. Have you read the labels of these "helpful" products? Many give poison-center phone numbers, toxic-waste disposal information, and disclaimers for allergic reactions, and for good reason. The ingredients of these products are poisonous, toxic, and downright hazardous—yet they're promoted as our very best housekeeping friends.

Raising a stink. I believe that many people resist cleaning chores because of the penetrating synthetic scents of most cleaning products. They not only smell bad, but for many people these products also cause shortened breath, burning eyes, headaches, and irritability. Couple these problems with subtle fears of toxicity, and it's no wonder homekeeping is maligned today.

What is the real cost of using these homekeeping products? I'd count indoor air pollution, solid and chemical toxic waste, and billions of dollars in unnecessary consumer spending. I wonder if the human cost is too high as well: Have consumers, impelled by advertising and ever more numerous products, become compulsive about cleaning everything, all the time? More human misery at the sponge mop isn't in our best interests.

A gentle proposal. Is there a better way? Of course there is! And I have found it to be a satisfying, economical, and ecological way too! Why not simplify your homekeeping needs? Why not learn how to incorporate the sensual, healing effects of the herbal world into your own homekeeping cupboard of favorite household formulations?

Over the past two years, I have evolved the ideas and formulations that I present in this book. With the help of the beloved world of herbs, I have turned my own homekeeping tasks into an herbal art that gives me great satisfaction and joy. I hope that these simple, effective herbal formulas will bring the same happiness to you.

CHAPTER 1
CENTURIES OF SCRUBBING

The history of homekeeping surely began before history was recorded. About half a million years ago, about when humans began to use fire and develop simple tools, chipped, sharp-edged stones appear throughout the ancient archaeological record. They were probably used for hunting and butchering, say the experts. I think ancient people also used these tools to scrape crud away and shape wooden trowels and diggers for burying smelly, rotting things. Antelope jaw bones with protruding teeth may have been weapons, it's true, but they could have been used to comb stones and grit from the hair of animal robes used as bedding.

Just imagine this prehistoric homekeeping scene. Rabbit skins were filled with cattail fur and tied around babies' bottoms—the first disposable diapers. Cedar boughs and fragrant grasses were lashed with sinew and used for comfortable mats. Sweeping and fire-fanning implements were made with thick reeds and hung from outcropped rocks on cave wall entrances. Horsetail reeds were bound together in bundles and used for scrubbing yuck off stone, wood, and bone implements. One-inch sticks, lashed into lattice flats with rawhide and hung from trees, became the cleaning racks for hide rugs, which women washed in the rain and dried in the sun.

It may have been the gender's heightened sense of smell and sensitivity to repulsive things that began a long history of female specialization in homekeeping. When the sea-going hunters of southern Europe 15,000 years ago were inventing the harpoon, the women were at home inventing the loom, the hanging storage basket, subterranean food storage, improved latrine facilities, bone needles, the stone oven, and botany. Feminine interest in shrubs, trees, vines, flowers, and herbs expanded over the centuries, eventually forming the basis for the specialties of medicine, religion, culinary arts, education, crafts, and magic.

Medieval Europeans routinely spread fragrant herbs upon the floors of cottages and castles for the pleasure of the scent; tansy, wormwood, lavender, and rosemary were used in this way. Sweet-smelling calamus reeds were appreciated so much that they were strewn on church floors for holy-day ceremonies. Unfortunately, these herbs often concealed unsanitary conditions and promoted the increase of vermin, including rats. Cleanliness of home and person became important in Europe only after the horror of the Black Death, or plague, appeared in about 1350. Although the disease killed about a third of the European population, its cause and method of transmission were not fully understood for another 500 years.

Modern Times. Homekeeping for health gained importance in the late 1800s, with Louis Pasteur's discovery of bacteria and viruses. Although Pasteur's "germ theory" was not immediately accepted, it set the stage for the original Mrs. Clean, Mrs. Isabella Beeton of London, who determined in 1861 to remedy the "discomfort and suffering" in households that practiced "untidy ways". In *Beeton's Book of Household Management,* she provided formulas for cleansers, polishes, and medicines along with many recipes and menus. Emphasizing justice, industriousness, cleanliness, and thrift, Mrs. Beeton established a long-lived standard. Nearly every cookbook published through the mid-twentieth century includes home cleaning formulations and recommendations, and to this day women are judged, at least to some extent, by the cleanliness of their homes.

At the same time, other cultures around the globe were maintaining fine and often artful levels of homekeeping, often with the help of various plants and herbs. These healthful practices had been developed over thousands of years. Danish women, for instance, became famous worldwide for their well-kept homes and keen attention to order and cleanliness. Their rhythmic systems of homekeeping endure today in the social culture of their tidy descendents. Likewise, Dutch women turned keeping house to an art form.

A Second American Revolution. In the early part of the twentieth century, Americans could purchase for the first time one-pound bars of plain, white, unscented household soap. For households with money to spend, this all-purpose cleanser, made from fat and lye, removed soap making from the chore list.

More importantly, however, those plain soap bars foretold the marketing explosion of "technologically advanced" gadgetry—sprays, spritzes, pastes, aerosols, powders, soaps, cleansing creams, caustics, detergents, disinfectants, secret agents, and hungry enzymes designed to devour dirt, grass stains, chocolate, pen marks, and the money in your pocket. Since the end of

World War II, literally thousands of products for home cleanliness have been brought to market.

Throughout this century of change, women kept house. They won the vote and scrubbed. They bobbed their hair, shortened their skirts, and cleaned. During the Depression, many struggled to keep the farm while keeping the house tidy, too. During World War II, Rosie not only riveted but rendered the floors spotless. So it is today: an unprecedented percentage of women take home paychecks— and take many loads of wash to the laundry room, too.

Advertisers for contemporary cleaning products have been quick to observe that women respond to promises that home cleaning products will save time and effort, easing the demands of the "liberated" lifestyle. Two incomes allow families to acquire more— more things to store, to clean, to polish and scrub. Manufacturers, of course, offer special products for all these purposes. The drive for affluence has eaten up free time, diluted family life, and piled on more obligations while filling our homes with stuff to clean—and stuff to clean stuff with.

A Big Turnaround. This book is about taking steps to stop this discouraging cycle. Homekeeping need not be a dreary chore; it need not empty your stores of energy along with your purse. Homekeeping shouldn't take up too much of your free time.

Instead, this book is about simplifying your cleaning chores in a way that makes them—dare we say it?—downright delightful. By making your own simple, herbal cleaning products, you can have a home that smells fresh, sparkles with cleanliness, and satisfies your desire for a healthful, pleasant environment. Along the way, you can experience contentment, creativity, and living lightly on the planet. By making and using your own herbal homekeeping products, you take an important step toward simplicity.

CHAPTER 2
RHYTHM, SYNERGY, AND SATISFACTION

In the overall scheme of homekeeping, I've found that attention to rhythm gives rise to synergy, and synergy to satisfaction. Establishing a pleasant rhythm helps you move along and gain momentum in your work. Not by chance are work songs from the railroad and mining industries deeply rhythmic; today, military marching chants connect rhythmic sound to movement, which helps people get the job done.

Consider the rhythm of your own movement: The lifting, bending, stooping, and sweeping motions of cleaning can be fashioned into a rhythmic sort of dance, one that is relaxed and fluid. Some homekeepers enjoy listening to music while they work. Others like to sing, giving homekeeping an energizing and healing dimension. Still others prefer silence interrupted only by the swish of the cleaning cloth.

Larger rhythms affect homekeeping—the passing of the days, weeks, months, and seasons. Some chores should be done every day; others about once a week. If you make up a calendar of such tasks, along with those that require monthly and seasonal attention, you will find that your homekeeping tasks fall into a natural, coherent rhythm.

The Danish Way. My Danish mother and aunts taught me the meaning of the seasons according to age-old Danish homekeeping customs. Everyday cleaning and weekly cleaning go on, of course, but Danish homekeepers clean the home from top to bottom early in the spring and again in late autumn.

Each month, a particular room in the home gets special attention. Walls, windows, and furniture are thoroughly cleaned, as are floor and window coverings. The homekeeper empties the storage area and sorts and reorganizes the contents, paying attention to the details. For instance, in the dining room, the napkin rings are organized, the candles sorted, and the crystal and silver polished. At the end of the month, the room is spotless, and it's time to begin with another area.

I like the Danish way of rotating cleaning jobs. It helps narrow down the tasks and spread them out. I don't have to try to clean *all* the closets in the house at once, just one. If I don't feel like washing windows, I can take care of a couple of drawers instead. Over the period of a month, I get it all done.

SYNERGY

Synergy means two or more achieving more than either can do alone. It works in chemistry, in physics, and in homekeeping. When one person in the household takes on all the homekeeping, rising tension is inevitable; so is haphazard cleanliness. When that load is divided and truly shared, however, synergy occurs.

By setting a rhythm and encouraging routines and habits among the members of your household, all involved can let go of the anxieties, guilt, and resentments that are often suffered in the name of a clean home. And two or more sharing the work with goodwill and camaraderie will create a better life for all. How can this be done?

Sheer will and determination! *Somebody* must take the bull by the horns and forge agreements with household members and establish the rhythms for homekeeping. (It will probably be you, since you are the one who is reading this book). Follow up on those commitments until good homekeeping habits become established throughout the household.

Divvy up the household chores. Our daily chores are well defined and divided among family members, but we do take into account special talents. For instance, my husband vacuums rugs better than anyone else I've ever known. When he was a boy, he and his father vacuumed every week, and maybe he likes the smell of the cedar oil drops that I put in cleaner bag, too. Whatever it is, it works! He does the vacuuming while I tend to other tasks. We both supervise the children's individual chores; at ages five and nine, they are able to do many housekeeping tasks well.

We set aside Friday evening or Saturday morning for our weekly homekeeping time. Everyone pitches in. When we have guests, they usually want to join in as well, and they often comment on how satisfying and how much fun it is to work with our family team.

Our guests usually ask how we've managed to get our children to help around the house without complaining and balking. The truth is, my husband and I have worked on this goal for a long time. I reply, "We started early and stayed with a consistent rhythm. We made a habit of working together, and we don't allow whining." Not even from ourselves!

We've also never given our children money or treats or special privileges in return for cleaning; their chores are part of their family duty. Instead, they understand that living in a pleasant home as a member of a co-operative family is a big reward in and of itself, one each of us earns every week.

Make tasks enjoyable. We use the herbal products in this book for cleaning our home because we don't want to expose anyone to the toxic ingredients in many commercial cleaning products. When a safe, effective, organic formula does the same job, why use a product that may cause more problems than it solves?

These products smell good and work well. No one must hold their breath against the fumes, open a window during a blizzard to provide ventilation while cleaning, or wear rubber gloves up to the elbow to avoid skin contact. Instead, these gentle products lighten the work load with pleasant scents and effective action.

Satisfaction

Satisfaction is a state of body and mind free from anger, anxiety, clutter, and grime. I spoke with many people about cleaning as I wrote this book, and most told me that despite their resistance to homekeeping tasks, these activities actually help them to work away anxiety and creatively solve problems. A few hours of cleaning not only renews the home, but one's resolve and purpose. This is especially true if I go about my cleaning deliberately; the more thoughtful and purposeful my manner, the greater the satisfaction.

SECRETS FOR INCREASING YOUR HOMEKEEPING SATISFACTION

Allow plenty of time so you won't feel rushed.

Drink a tall glass of cool water before you begin, in the middle, and again at the end of your cleaning time.

Open the windows and let in some fresh air while you work.

Try some gentle stretches to warm your muscles before you begin to clean. Stretch your arms, shoulders, and legs to help prevent the soreness that sometimes follows vigorous homekeeping. When you have finished, stretch again and relax deeply.

Burn a little dried sage, cedar, or sweetgrass before you begin and after you finish. The smoke removes odor from the air; in some cultures, these herbs are the basis of purification rituals.

Experiment with sound—classical music, rock 'n roll, easy listening—while you work.

Try silence.

As you work, focus on deep, rhythmic movements.

Breathe deeply and regularly as you carry out your tasks; when you use herbal products, you won't need to hold your breath against the chemicals as you do with many manufactured products.

As you clean and polish wood, think about the life of the tree.

When you're cleaning clay, stones, plastics, and metals, consider their origins in the Earth. Let yourself feel gratitude for these materials that make up the body of your home.

Lightly scent your home by placing a cotton ball containing a few drops of herbal essential oil in an open window.

CHAPTER 3
HERBAL HOMEKEEPING

There are twenty bad reasons why I'm writing this chapter: ammonia, bleach, butyl cellosolve, cresol, dye, ethanol, formaldehyde, glycol, hydrochloric acid, hydrofluoric acid, lye, napthalene, paradichlorobenzenes, perchloroethylene, petroleum distillates, phenol, phosphoric acid, propellants, sulfuric acid, and trichloroethylene.

I found these chemicals listed on the labels of cleaning formulas. All are dangerous and most are considered hazardous waste. Are they fun to use? No! Effective? You bet—but they cost plenty, both in dollars and risk to the environment.

Here are the *good* reasons for this chapter, along with descriptions of the ways they benefit homekeeping.

Baking soda (sodium bicarbonate), a mild alkali that is useful in a variety of cleaning applications. (Don't confuse this with washing soda, also called sal soda, which is not the same substance.)

White vinegar, a slightly acidic liquid, is useful in many cleaning formulas. (Heinz vinegar is made from grains, but many others are made from nonrenewable petroleum alcohols, so I prefer Heinz.)

Sodium lauryl sulfate powder (SLS) is a simple, safe, and effective detergent derived from coconut oil. Its power to clean surfaces is stronger than that of soap. You can order SLS powder by mail from suppliers listed in the Resource Directory at the end of the book.

Unscented bulk castile soap, like SLS, serves as a surfactant by helping to loosen and wash away dirt. A several-pound bar that can be grated into formulas when needed is very handy. It's available by mail-order; see the Resource Directory.

Lemon, lime, and **grapefruit** juices, fresh or in concentrate, do more than smell great— they're acidic and antibacterial and make a lively addition to any cleaning formula.

Borax (sodium bromate) is a mildly alkaline, water-soluble salt. It loosens dirt and stains while removing odors. Borax is usually available in supermarkets, but it's offered by mail, too.

Carnauba and **olive oils** are excellent additions to wood cleaners because they recondition and polish the surfaces.

Beeswax turns formulas into pastes for waxing and shining.

Lanolin, a natural oil extracted from wool, restores some of the fiber's natural sheen and water repellence when added to wool-washing soaps.

Clay powder is a very mild abrasive. It also easily absorbs essential oils and makes them easier to disperse in powdered cleaning formulas.

Pumice is finely ground volcanic rock; add it as an abrasive to scrubbing compounds for big jobs.

MORE GOOD REASONS: ESSENTIAL OILS

Distilled from plant roots, rinds, flowers, seeds, and resins, essential oils are highly concentrated and intensely scented. For homekeeping, they offer important cleaning and disinfectant benefits.

Some essential oil scents lift the spirits. An entire field of study, aromatherapy, deals with the healing potential of aromas. It's based on the idea that the human olfactory nerves lead directly to the brain's emotional center, the limbic system, so perhaps one's emotional well-being can be improved by the judicious use of scents.

I think aromatherapy works, and I like to employ its principles in homekeeping. These are my favorite essential oils for cleaning. They are effective, easy to obtain, and not too expensive. A little goes a long way!

Lavender oil is a disinfectant. Its calming scent is often used by aromatherapists to ease tension, anxiety, and depression.

Lemon, orange and grapefruit oils are tough degreasers with refreshing clean scents that can alleviate depression and fatigue.

Eucalyptus oil disinfects while helping relieve stuffy noses. It's an excellent cleaning choice if you are fighting off a cold!

Tea tree oil, distilled from the Australian *Melaleuca alternifolia* tree, is effective against bacteria, fungus, and some viruses; it's terrific for cleaning when there's illness in the home. Inhaling tea-tree's strong scent eases congestion.

White cedar oil disinfects and provides an uplifting scent. It's another good choice when illness is present.

Lime oil has a lighthearted citrus scent that is so delicious, it's easy to forget how well it performs as a degreaser and general cleanser. In a pinch, mix a few drops of this oil with a couple of tablespoons of baking soda for a slightly abrasive kitchen scrub.

Pine oil is a fine old standby for homekeepers. This plentiful and inexpensive essential oil is a degreaser and a bit of a disinfectant. Its clean, outdoor scent stimulates alertness—sometimes helpful during cleaning.

Essential oils are not the same as the synthetic scent oils that you can find at, say, crafts stores. Such chemically contrived oils don't originate from plants, and they cannot offer the cleaning and therapeutic benefits of essential oils.

When using essential oils, remember that they are highly concentrated and as a rule should not be applied directly to skin or to household surfaces. Never ingest essential oils; should this happen by accident, do not induce vomiting; seek immediate medical help.

CREATING A GENTLE CLEANING CUPBOARD

The next time your plastic broom falls apart, try a wooden-handled one made with real broom grass. Enjoy the beautiful natural color of the broom grass; imagine dancing in a field of waving grass as you sweep. Plastic just can't elicit such beautiful images and escapes. Retired plastic brooms are doomed to haunt the landfill for eternity, but natural brooms can be buried in the Earth to rot into the great cycle of life.

For economy and performance, cleaning cloths of cotton, hemp, and lint-free linen beat paper towels hands down. Natural sponges are fun and durable, and if you like creative cleaning imagery, what could be better than the ocean home of your sponge to set the stage?

Cotton mops with wooden handles are far superior to synthetic sponge mops. Big cotton mops are cumbersome, so I lop off about three inches of the floppy yarn. Like natural brooms, cotton mops that have ended their purposeful lives can be laid to rest with dignity.

I wasn't going to tell you this, but I even have a wooden bucket! I bought it years ago from a cooper—a barrel maker—at a crafts fair. It's watertight, lightweight, and longer lasting than a plastic pail. The more I use it, the prettier it becomes.

I also have a peacock-feather duster and a wooden stick with sheep's wool attached that I use for dusting and cleaning corners. Both can be rinsed clean. For some clean-up jobs, a natural whisk broom works just as well as a hand-held vacuum. To clean floors and carpets, I use a handy non-electric mechanical carpet sweeper that's effective and economical. I like its peaceful little purr more than the roar of a heavy electric vacuum.

What more do you need? An old toothbrush, a razor blade in a holder, and natural-bristle brushes with wooden handles for tubs and toilets. These simple cleaning tools will do the job in a way that will make you proud.

OTHER USEFUL EQUIPMENT

To make your herbal cleaning formulas, you'll need measuring cups and spoons, wide-mouth and narrow funnels. Use large stainless steel or glass bowls rather than ceramic or plastic ones that may absorb essential oil scents.

Gather up an assortment of spray bottles, squirt bottles, and shakers with flip tops (one of my favorites is an old parmesan cheese container). Assorted jars or plastic storage tubs are handy, too. All these will be used to store your products. For labeling the containers, you'll need labels, markers, and tape.

CHAPTER 4
RECIPES FOR GENERAL CLEANING

Eucalyptus, Lavender, and Tea Tree Spray Cleaner

This spray cleaner has a triple crew to disinfect surfaces, wipe out mold, and discourage its return. Eucalyptus, lavender, and tea tree are all known for their antimicrobial properties. Together, they smell exquisitely clean, and they know how to get the job done.

1 teaspoon sodium lauryl sulfate
1 teaspoon borax
2 tablespoons white vinegar
2 cups hot water
1/4 teaspoon eucalyptus essential oil
1/4 teaspoon lavender essential oil
3 drops tea tree essential oil

Mix all ingredients together and stir until dry ingredients dissolve. Pour into spray bottle for use and long-term storage. To use, spray as needed on any surface except glass. Scrub and rinse with a clean, damp cloth.

Carnauba and Lavender Furniture Wax

This paste wax will clean, condition, and polish wood surfaces while providing a protective coat of wax. Fine carnauba wax is derived from the leaves of the palm tree *Copernica cerifera.*

This formula is lightly scented with lavender essential oil, which enhances its cleaning power. Use a circular motion to rub it onto wooden floors and antique furniture, buff with sheep's wool and a soft cotton cloth, then enjoy the peaceful calm offered by the scent of lavender and the soft glow of the polished wood.

1/4 cup carnauba wax
2 tablespoons beeswax
1 1/4 cup olive oil
1 teaspoon lavender essential oil

Melt waxes over low heat in small saucepan. Stir in olive oil, then lavender oil. Pour mixture into a container of tin, plastic, or glass and allow to harden.

Lavender-Ginger Suds
Upholstery Cleaner and Rug Shampoo

This is a high-suds cleaner. It's actually the suds and scrubbing (provided by you) that do the tandem job of lifting the dirt and smells from rugs and plush furniture. The lavender and ginger essential oils will help if animal smells are a problem.

Before tackling the entire job, test-clean any light or unusual fabrics—better safe than sorry! And remember not to soak your furniture; use only the suds for cleaning.

4 cups water
1 cup white vinegar
3 tablespoons sodium lauryl sulfate
2 teaspoons baking soda
1/8 teaspoon lavender essential oil
1/8 teaspoon ginger essential oil

Mix all ingredients together and fill a handheld rug/upholstery shampoo bottle half full. Shake the bottle vigorously and shampoo your furniture or rug using small circular motions. Try not to penetrate fabrics with much more than a thin layer of suds, but scrub the sudsy area well.

Lemon-Mint Window Wash

If you live where flies routinely cause problems in the summer, you'll love this recipe. Your windows will be sparkling clean, and the fresh lemon juice and peppermint oil in the formula discourages the pesky critters from perching on your windows again.

Before you wash the windows, whisk away dust and dead bugs from the casing using a small, handheld broom. For the shiniest windows, use sheets of newspaper (black and white only) to scrub and shine them. The newspaper ink may darken your hands, but it shines the windows without streaking.

Juice from one fresh lemon
2 cups water or club soda
1/2 teaspoon peppermint essential oil
1 teaspoon cornstarch

Mix all ingredients and pour into plastic spray bottle.
Shake well before using.

Lemon Metal Cleaner

No need to buy four different metal cleaners and keep them locked up under the sink, or to subject your sinuses, lungs, and eyes to the stinging, burning sensation that most metal cleaners cause. This simple formula will clean any metal except aluminum. To clean aluminum, substitute cream of tarter for baking soda and omit the salt.

Fresh squeezed juice of 2 lemons
1/3 cup baking soda
1 teaspoon fine salt
6 tablespoons clay powder

Mix all ingredients together until you have a paste. Add water or more clay if needed for consistency.

Rub paste onto metal with extremely fine steel wool and allow to sit for fifteen minutes. Wash off with a sponge and clear water. Polish the metal with a soft piece of felt, flannel, or sheep wool. For stubborn tarnish, repeat the process.

CHAPTER 5
THE KITCHEN AND BATH

Key Lime Dish Detergent Powder

Given the sheer volume of dirty dishes generated by the average household, this is probably the most ecologically important recipe in this book. Powdered dish detergent eliminates the need for buying plastic bottles and then recycling or disposing of them. The weight of the water included in dishwashing liquid need not be shipped from coast to coast, saving fuel and air pollution. Washing dishes in the sink saves electricity and water, too.

This powder is just as effective as liquid. If you find that you really prefer a liquid, add some boiling water to the formula, stir until the powder is dissolved, and bottle in your favorite squirt dispenser. The following formula will last the average family of four approximately six months.

1/2 cup clay powder
2 tablespoons lime essential oil
24 cups sodium lauryl sulfate
6 cups baking soda

Wear a dust mask to mix this formula. Mix clay powder and essential oil, then, in a two-gallon pail or container, combine with the baking soda and sodium lauryl sulfate. Mix well.

To convert to liquid soap, add 18 cups of boiling water and stir until all ingredients are dissolved. Store in gallon jugs and refill squirt bottles as needed.

To use, add about a tablespoon of powder or a good squirt of liquid per sink load while filling the sink. For tough jobs, make a paste of the powder by adding water and rub directly on the spot, or apply the liquid directly to it.

Eucalyptus-Mint All-Purpose Disinfecting Soft Soap for Kitchen and Bath

This soap can be used for dishes, handwashing, floors, stoves, refrigerators, sinks, and hands. It's mild to the skin but effective enough to get cleaning jobs done. The eucalyptus and mint provide a disinfecting quality as well as a fresh scent; any areas washed with this soap will be undesirable to crawling insects and flies. They'll stay away for quite a while.

5 cups grated castile soap
1/2 cup baking soda
1 teaspoon borax
6 cups hot peppermint tea
1 teaspoon eucalyptus essential oil

Put grated soap into a 3-quart stainless steel saucepan and add hot mint tea. Simmer for fifteen minutes on low heat. Add baking soda, borax, and eucalyptus oil. Store in a labeled plastic jug or squirt bottle. Shake before using.

Grapefruit Abrasive Cleanser

This cleanser gets its punch from finely ground pumice, a volcanic rock dust. It's comparable to a soft scrub and can be used for tubs, sinks, tiles, and even hardworking hands that have been stained with grease. The lingering scent is pungent and fresh!

1 cup fine-grade pumice
1/2 cup clay powder
2 tablespoons grapefruit essential oil
1/4 cup baking soda
1/3 cup sodium lauryl sulfate
1/ 2 cup boiling water (or enough to make a thick paste)

Mix all ingredients together and stir. Store in a labeled airtight container with a label.

To use, apply gently with a damp sponge or cloth and scrub. Use a light touch on fiberglass fixtures.

Russian Dishwashing Disk

A physician in our community spent several months volunteering in a Russian childbirth clinic last year. He brought home many interesting stories, but to me, the story of the Russian dishwashing bar was the best! In Russia, dishwashing involves a solid soap disk and a dishwashing brush that resembles American vegetable brushes. The sink is filled with hot water, but the soap is brushed onto the dishes rather than added to the water. Having made this soap and tried it out, I really like the whole process. It's simple and useful.

1 cup grated castile soap
1 tablespoon boiling water
1 tablespoon sodium lauryl sulfate
1 teaspoon lemon essential oil

Put grated castile soap in a plastic container with a lid and sprinkle the soap with sodium lauryl sulfate and lemon oil. Add boiling water. Cover and let sit for ten minutes.

Form the soap into a ball and then flatten it to form a disk. The soap I made is donut-shaped to fit a special handmade bowl, which has a center post so the soap doesn't slide about and a wide lip to minimize splashes. Whether you make a donut or a disk, let the soap air-dry for several days.

Place the disk in a container near the sink. To use it, swipe the brush across the disk and apply the soap directly to what you're washing.

Toilet Bowl Cleaners

I cleaned my first toilet at age twelve, and cleaned at least one more nearly every week for the next twenty-seven years. My feelings have ranged from disgust to resignation, but the big question has always been, "Why am I the ONLY person in my home who cares about having this clean?"

Now I spritz and spray and swish away to the tune of my own happy whistle. No more resentment! I wouldn't share this job with anyone—not even if they begged!

Well, not really—and probably no one will be begging me for this job any time soon. But why waste time in unhappy resignation when a better way exists?

Spritz-and-Spray Toilet Bowl Cleaner

The baking soda and vinegar in this formula dissolve mineral buildup, while the oils loosen grime and give a fresh, clean scent.

1/2 teaspoon sodium lauryl sulfate
2 tablespoons baking soda
2 tablespoons vinegar
1 teaspoon orange essential oil
1 teaspoon grapefruit essential oil
2 cups water

Mix all ingredients in a 4-cup measuring cup or a bowl. When you mix the vinegar and baking soda, it will foam. Let this mixture stand for 10 minutes before pouring into a spray bottle.

Blue Angel Swirl Toilet Bowl Cleaner

If you prefer a powder for cleaning toilets, you'll like this formula.

1 teaspoon lime essential oil
1 teaspoon grapefruit essential oil
2 tablespoons clay powder
3 tablespoons sodium lauryl sulfate
12 tablespoons borax
8 tablespoons baking soda
11/2 teaspoons ultramarine powder (coloring agent)

Mix essential oils with clay powder in a bowl using a small whisk or fork. Add other ingredients and stir until well-blended. Store in a labeled plastic container.

Use 1 tablespoon per bowl. For stubborn stains, wet the powder so it resembles a paste, apply to the stain, and allow to sit for several hours before flushing.

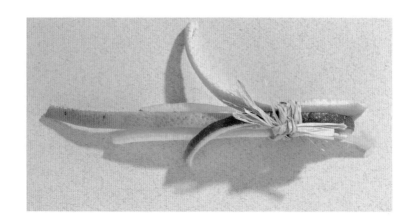

CHAPTER 6
LEATHER CARE

Beeswax Saddle Soap

Harness, saddle, and bridle leathers should be completely cleaned and conditioned at least twice a year to extend their usefulness. In fact, all types of leathers would last longer if they got this luxurious treatment.

2 tablespoons beeswax
1/2 cup olive oil
1 cup grated castile soap
1/4 teaspoon lavender or tea tree essential oils (optional: to prevent mold and mildew)

Melt beeswax into olive oil on low heat. Add grated castile soap and stir until well melted. Pour into shallow plastic container or lidded tin. Let cool before using.

To apply, scoop up a small amount of saddle soap and rub onto leather in a circular motion, using a sponge or a piece of loofah sponge. Rinse with a wrung-out, damp cotton cloth. Allow leather to dry completely before conditioning.

Boot and Saddle Conditioner

This conditioner helps keep leather supple and shed water while it adds a polished look. I usually treat my leather goods to an application every winter, spring, and fall. Though nice, its smell repels mice, raccoons, porcupines, and other little beasts who love to chew on salty leather.

This formula always travels with me on wilderness trips, too; if the weather turns rainy, I use it to keep dampness out.

3/4 cup olive oil
3/8 cup castor oil
1/4 cup beeswax
1/4 cup carnauba wax
1/4 teaspoon lavender, tea tree, or eucalyptus essential oil
(optional; to prevent mold and mildew)

Melt all ingredients over low heat and stir well. Pour into shallow flat container with a lid. Cool and label.

To use, rub into leather with a cloth or piece of loofah sponge. Let dry and polish gently.

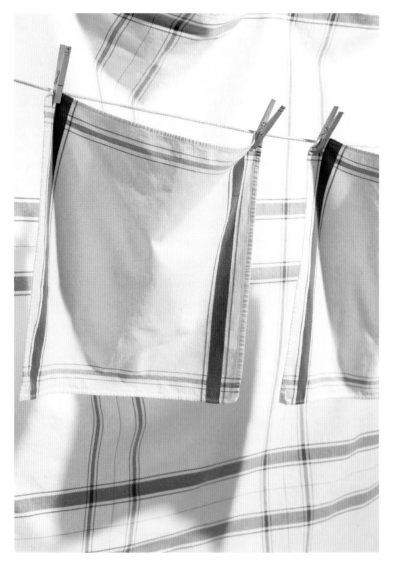

CHAPTER 7
THE LAUNDRY

Once-a-Year Laundry Concentrate

Life will be better with this simple and effective formula for the laundry in your life and you'll run out of laundry powder only once a year. You won't be rushing to the store on short notice, filling the trashcans with plastic or paperboard containers, or wondering if your laundry powder damages the environment.

The following formula will last a year for an average family of four that generates five loads of wash per week for twelve months. Make more or less according to your needs.

1/4 cup clay powder
2–3 tablespoons essential oil of your choice
13 cups borax
12 cups baking soda
4 cups sodium lauryl sulfate

You may want to use a dust mask or tie a scarf over your nose and mouth when mixing this formula.

Using a small whisk or fork, mix the clay powder with the essential oil. Add the remaining ingredients and mix well in a 2- or 3-gallon pail. Use 1/8 cup of laundry powder per load.

Sweetly Scented Soft Soap

Before detergents were invented, women used soft soap for laundering. Soft soap, usually a batch of hard soap gone bad, was made with wood-ash lye, water, and animal fats. It was strictly utilitarian and unscented, and often somewhat on the caustic side. Thus soft soap had an extra cleaning kick for laundry, floors, walls, and dishes, but it was unkind to skin.

This updated soft soap smells divine and is gentle on the skin. Although it produces few bubbles, its cleaning power is outstanding. If used regularly, it will likely leave a little soap residue in your washer and on your clothes, so add 1/2 cup of white vinegar to your rinse cycle. This formula is highly recommended for people who have sensitivities to detergents.

12 cups grated castile soap
12 cups boiling water
1 cup baking soda
1/4 cup borax
1 teaspoon lemon essential oil
1 teaspoon grapefruit essential oil

Put grated soap into a two-gallon stainless kettle. Add boiling water, simmer, and stir frequently for 15 minutes, then stir in other ingredients.

Use 1 cup per load of clothes or as needed for household cleaning.

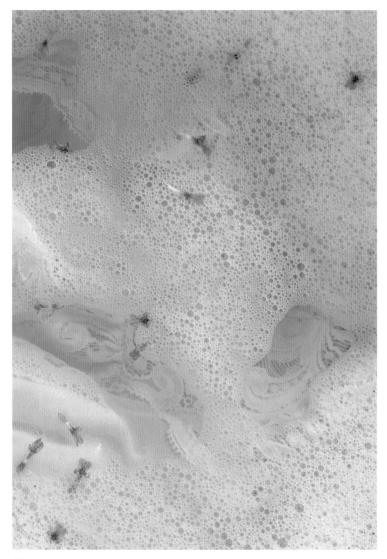

Delicate Garment Soap with Lavender

I have always enjoyed hand washing my most delicate clothing. With my lavender soap I prepare a sink full of warm, sudsy water, then immerse the garments slowly, one at a time. I gently lift them in and out of the water, protecting the lace and tiny seams while enjoying the soft swish of the water and the wafting scent of lavender flowers. When my special clothes are rinsed, I let them dry outdoors; the bees often visit to enjoy the lavender fragrance that lingers.

8 tablespoons sodium lauryl sulfate
4 tablespoons grated castile soap
2 teaspoons clay powder
1/4 teaspoon lavender oil

Mix clay and lavender oil with a small whisk or fork. Add remaining ingredients and blend at high speed in a blender. (This will not ruin your blender for food use). Store in a plastic container.

To use, sprinkle 1 tablespoon of powder into a sink of warm water and swish the water until the powder is dissolved. Then add garments and wash; rinse thoroughly and dry.

SPOT-REMOVER BASICS

Stain removal can be tricky. Here are some general considerations.

Timing is essential. Treat the stain as soon as possible, before it has a chance to soak into fabric or dry.

Most stains should be rinsed in icy cold water, especially protein-based stains such as milk, grease, or blood. Hot water tends to set the stain in the fabric and make it practically permanent.

Commercial stain removers can remove the dye from fabrics that are not colorfast, so test your fabric before treating a stain. Apply a drop of the stain remover and follow manufacturer's instructions. If the dye comes out, don't use it on a larger area.

Tangerine Dream Spot Remover

Tangerine Dream Spot Remover paste uses tangerine oil to dissolve the stain, sodium lauryl sulfate to lift the stain and wash it away, and borax to boost cleaning power. Use this spot remover on tough grease, ink, chocolate, and blood stains.

1 tablespoon tangerine essential oil (or any citrus essential oil)
4 tablespoons glycerin
2 tablespoons borax
1 teaspoon sodium lauryl sulfate

Mix the essential oil with the glycerin; then add the remaining ingredients. Store the spot remover in a small labeled plastic or glass container.

To use, first rinse the stain with cold water, removing as much of the stain as possible. Then apply the paste to the stain and rub for several minutes and rinse again. Repeat if necessary.

Sleepy-Bye Soap for Bed Linens

This soap is one part extravagance and all pleasure. Bed sheets washed with this lavender-scented soap will soothe the longest, most difficult day. Why? Because lavender oil's scent has the power to calm the nerves and ease the mind. I enjoy hanging my sheets to dry on a shady outdoor line to preserve the lavender scent.

1/4 cup clay powder
2 tablespoons lavender essential oil
1 cup borax
2 cups baking soda
3/4 cup sodium lauryl sulfate

Mix clay powder with lavender oil in a 2-quart container, then stir in other ingredients. Use 1 cup of mixture per load of sheets. If desired, add 1/4 teaspoon lavender oil to rinse cycle.

Wool Wash with Lanolin and Cedar

This soft soap's mission is not only cleaning; it enhances and protects fabric, too. The lanolin in the formula restores wool to some of its original luster and water repellence; cedar essential oil keeps moths away.

Use this soap in the washer, on the delicate cycle with cool water. It's also great for handwashing your favorite woolens.

2 cups grated castile soap
6 cups boiling water
1 tablespoon sodium lauryl sulfate
1 teaspoon white cedar oil
1 teaspoon lanolin

Put grated soap into a wide mouth 1/2 gallon jug (glass or heavy plastic). Add the boiling water and let the mixture sit for half an hour; then stir in other ingredients. Store in a capped jar.

Use approximately 1/4 cup per sink load of woolens or 1 cup per automatic load.

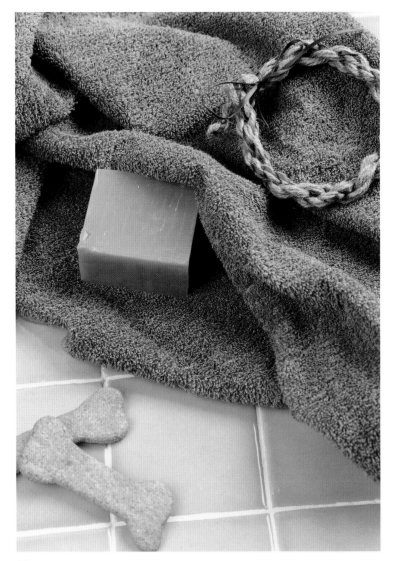

CHAPTER 8
CATS, DOGS, AND HORSES

Herbal Flee Flea Shampoo, Oil, and Collar for Dogs and Cats

My dog Cloud hated her summer flea baths, and so did I; at that time fighting fleas required toxins galore. Which was worse, the baths or the fleas? For a long time, it was a toss-up. Expensive flea baths, collars, sprays, powders and dips are heavily laced with chemicals that are potentially harmful to pets, people, and the environment. Fleas, on the other hand, make pets and people miserable with their bites and can carry disease and parasites, too.

Following are some healthy herbal alternatives for flea control, all based on the herbal Flee Flea formula that I developed. Flee Flea pet oil and my pet shampoos have been used and loved by my two- and four-legged customers for years. The Flee Flea formula has been approved for safety by the Environmental Protection Agency and is legally considered a repellant. I hope you and your pet will enjoy natural flea control. The birds, bees, and fish will thank you, too.

Flee Flea Oil

2 tablespoons peppermint essential oil
1/2 cup plus 2 tablespoons rosemary essential oil
2 tablespoons white cedar essential oil
1/4 cup citronella essential oil
2 tablespoons eucalyptus essential oil
3/4 cup olive oil

Mix all ingredients well and store in labeled opaque bottle. Apply 1 to 2 teaspoons of oil to your hands and rub together, then apply all over your dog's or cat's body every three days during flea season. Wash hands with soap and water after application. Do not get into eyes of pets or humans. Do not take internally. Wash your pet every 7 to 14 days with Flee Flea Shampoo.

Herbal Flee Flea Shampoo

2 cups boiling water (or, if you have access to fresh tansy, make
2 cups strong tansy tea and use in place of the water)
1/2 cup sodium lauryl sulfate
1/4 cup white vinegar
1/8 cup Flee Flea Oil

Mix water and sodium lauryl sulfate together and stir until com-
pletely dissolved. Cool. Mix vinegar and Flee Flea Oil together and
add to other ingredients. Combine well and store in an opaque
bottle, carefully labeled.

To use, place pet in tub and dampen the coat. Pour a tablespoon or
more of the shampoo into your palm, rub hands together, and
lather, beginning in front of the ears and working back and down,
until the pet's coat is saturated with the shampoo. Rinse well.

Flee Flea Flea Collar

I recommend removing the flea collar at night to offer your pet a break from the strong herbal scents.

2 tablespoons peppermint essential oil
1/2 cup plus 2 tablespoons rosemary essential oil
2 tablespoons white cedar essential oil
1/4 cup citronella essential oil
2 tablespoons eucalyptus essential oil

To make your pet an herbal flea collar, measure a heavy cotton wick or a natural fiber rope that will tie comfortably around your pet's neck and slip off over its head should it become caught on a branch or fence. Soak the rope in Flee Flea Oil and let it dry for several hours. Then tie the collar around your pet's neck.

Resoak the flea collar every two weeks or as needed.

Aloe Vera and Comfrey-Mint Healing Shampoo for Dogs and Cats

Use this healing shampoo for pets with skin irritation. For pets with hot spots, apply fresh aloe vera juice to the spots twice a day for rapid healing.

2 cups strong comfrey and mint tea (still hot)
1/2 cup sodium lauryl sulfate
1/4 cup fresh aloe vera juice scraped from the insides of aloe vera leaves
1 tablespoon olive oil

Mix tea and sodium lauryl sulfate and stir until well dissolved. Add remaining ingredients and store in a labeled squirt bottle. Shake before using, apply as for flea shampoo above, and rinse the pet well.

Geranium Fly-Away Shampoo for Horses and Ponies

I developed this herbal formula to keep away deerflies, horse flies, and mosquitoes from my horses and my little old pony, Silver. It became the Equine Esssential Horse Shampoo Bar that is now sold through my mail-order company, SunFeather Natural Soap Company. If horses dislike the smell of this cleanser, they don't remark upon it.

This formula is approved as a legal and safe repellent by the Environmental Protection Agency.

1/2 cup sodium lauryl sulfate
2 cups boiling water
1 teaspoon lavender essential oil
1/8 teaspoon patchouli essential oil
1/8 teaspoon geranium essential oil

Mix well the sodium lauryl sulfate and boiling water, then add essential oils. Bottle in a labeled, opaque container and store in a cool place.

Wet the horse's coat and apply soap starting high on the neck. Work back and down to protect the horse's eyes. I save the plastic net bags from onions because they make gentle yet thorough scrubbers that the horses seem to enjoy. Rinse coat well.

CHAPTER 9
GARDEN, YARD, AND ORCHARD

Green and Clean Car Wash Soft Soap

This mild, kind soap will keep your car's exterior clean and shining. So beautiful will it be that birds will think twice before doing a dirty deed and bugs will hesitate to splatter on its windshield. The lingering scent of balsam will make washing the car a pleasure.

3 cups grated castile soap
1/2 cup sodium lauryl sulfate
3 cups boiling water
1 tablespoon borax
1 tablespoon balsam fir essential oil

Dissolve the soap and the sodium lauryl sulfate in the boiling water; add borax and essential oil and mix well. Label and store in a covered container.

To use, measure 1 1/2 cups of soft soap into a three-gallon pail; add two gallons of warm water and stir well. Use this solution to wash the car, stroking with a soft brush and rinsing with cool water. Pat dry.

Soapy Tobacco and Garlic Pest Spray

This formula terrifies garden insects. If you have access to fresh tansy, all the better—include it in the mix! This formula is most effective when fresh. A batch will keep in the refrigerator for up to two weeks, but please, please label it. It is vile-tasting stuff, and tansy should never be taken internally.

1 cup grated castile soap
1 cup coarsely chopped tobacco leaves, fresh or cured
3 cups boiling water, divided
1 entire bulb (not just one clove) garlic, peeled and crushed or chopped
1 cup of chopped fresh tansy (optional)

In a bowl, dissolve soap in 1 cup boiling water and set aside.

In blender jar, pour remainder of boiling water over tobacco leaves and let set for ten minutes or so. Add garlic and tansy (if available) and whirl until smooth. Strain through cheesecloth and discard solid materials. Add herbal liquid to soap mixture and stir; pour into a labeled spray bottle.

To use, spray the herbal liquid on insects and their environs at early morning and dusk for three days in a row. Because this mix drives most bugs away, but does not kill them, apply as needed.

Geranium Bug Oil

This formula was developed for people who don't care to use products containing deet, a chemical insect repellent whose safety has been questioned recently.

I have been told by ascended masters that biting insects can be dissuaded from their violence through benevolence and mental telepathy. I try this every year and find that it works extremely well during winter, but in summertime I put my faith in Geranium Bug Oil. I've tested it on wilderness hikers, loggers, and little children. It's safe, it works, and the EPA has approved it as an insect repellant.

2 tablespoons citronnella essential oil
2 tablespoons rosemary essential oil
2 tablespoons geranium essential oil
2 tablespoons eucalyptus essential oil
1/2 cup olive oil

Mix all oils together and store in a labeled opaque bottle. Dab oil on bandana, clothing, hat, and skin. Do not get into eyes or mouth.

Citrus Anti-Insect Air Spritzer

Instead of those bad-smelling aerosol poisons designed to oust bugs from the patio, porch, or yard, try this pleasant, safe, and economical spritzer.

At your local garden center, look for a bottle that will spray a very fine mist. Don't expect this formula to kill bugs on contact—it's not for eradicating them! Instead, it chases them away long enough for you to enjoy your picnic.

2 cups vodka
1 tablespoon citronella essential oil
1 tablespoon eucalyptus essential oil
1 teaspoon geranium essential oil
1 teaspoon rosemary essential oil
1 teaspoon orange essential oil
1 teaspoon lemon essential oil

Mix all ingredients in a glass jar and shake well. Pour into a labeled plastic spritzer bottle.

To use, spray a fine mist into the air where bugs are unwelcome.

Deer, Don't Eat My Fruit Trees

This discovery was made by St. Lawrence Nurseries. The owners of this specialty northern-climate nursery live near my soap company, and they decided to try some of our inexpensive scrap soap to repel deer from their orchards. I didn't have much faith in the idea, but I was sure wrong!

The owners hung small bundles of herbal soap scrap here and there on tree branches throughout the orchard. Their plan worked like a charm: The deer wouldn't come near the trees. As a bonus, the rain eventually melted the soap bundles, lending a bit of alkalinity to the soil below.

To repel deer, roll several pounds of soft, scented soap or soap scrap into balls. Tie the balls into small bundles, using cloth or net and string. Hang several bundles from each tree. If you make your own soap, you probably have scrap soap around the house. If not, you can mail order it inexpensively from SunFeather Natural Soap Company—we've got plenty!

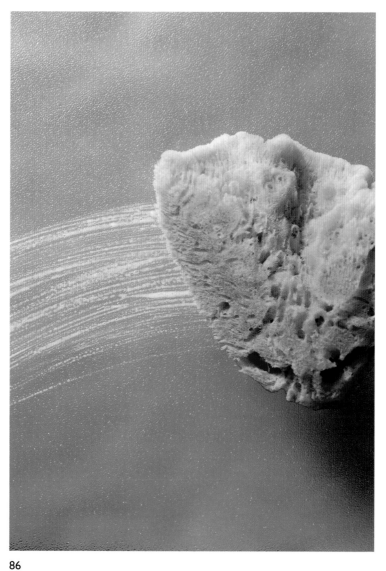

AFTERWORD
BREATHE DEEPLY, LIVE IN PEACE

Many of us in North America have been fooled by abundance. It has not brought us ease or joy; instead, our lives have become too complex to be healthy or fulfilling. We pay the price from our souls.

By living more simply we can increase our security financially, ecologically, and socially. By becoming more selective and thoughtful about the way we live, we free ourselves for families, friends, and learning—enhancing our joy and pleasuring our souls.

Simplicity is the act of saying no to too much and saying yes to matters of the heart, the land, and the family. I have written *Herbal Homekeeping* to help take you home to the beauty of simple endeavors using simple ingredients and Nature's simple herbs. So now, if you will, please go forth and simplify!

RESOURCE DIRECTORY

Clean Team
206 B North Main
Jackson, CA 95642
800-717-2532
www.thecleanteam.com
Tools, including ostrich-feather dusters, supplies, information

Frontier Herb Cooperative
Box 299
Norway, Iowa 52318
800-669-3275
Assorted raw materials

Fuller Brush Catalog, Inc.
P.O. Box 729
Great Bend, KS 67530
316-792-1711
Brushes and cleaning tools

Harmony
360 Interlochen Blvd.
Suite 300
Broomfield, CO 80021
800-456-1177
www.harmonycatalog.com
Products in harmony with the Earth

High Point Crafts
POB 105
Main Street
Fabius, NY 13063
315-683-5312
Individually handcrafted feather dusters made with naturally molted peacock and ostrich feathers, brooms with handles of sapling hardwood or forged iron, and additional traditional products.

Life on the Planet
23852 Pacific Coast Hwy #200
Malibu, CA 90265
818-880-5144
www.cleanhouse.com
Bottles for home cleaning formulas

Munro
POB 431777
Big Pine Key, FL 33043
305-872-8485
Hand-selected and professionally processed natural sponges for

kitchen, bath, shower, and auto-mobile washing. Choose 5-inch sheepswool, yellow, or seawool sponges or a package containing one of each.

Scheumack Broom Company
1025 Conger Street
Eugene, OR 97402
541-338-0502
Large selection of functional and durable handmade brooms, dust pans, walking sticks, and other products embellished with hand-carved wood spirits, animals, and other figures. Designs based on early American traditions.

Seeds of Simplicity
P.O. Box 9955
Glendale, California 91226
818-247-4332
www.slnet.com/cip/seeds
Simple-living curricula for children and information about forming simplicity circles for adults. Highly recommended!

Seventh Generation
49 Hercules Drive
Colchester, Vermont 05446
800-456-1191
Eco-home items and cleaning tools; catalog

SunFeather Natural Soap Company
1551 Hwy 72
Potsdam, NY 13676
www.sunsoap.com
315-265-3648 /full color catalog
Hand-crafted soaps and shampoos, soapmaking kits, books and supplies. Bulk castile soaps, essential oils, pumice, sodium lauryl sulfate, Soapmakers' Club, gazette, and home party plan.

TKB Trading
360 24th Street
Oakland, California 94612
www.tkbtrading.com
510-451-9011
Natural colorants, glycerin soap-making supplies

RECOMMENDED READING

Bau Breathnatch, S. *Simple Abundance: A Daybook of Comfort and Joy.* New York: Warner Books, 1995.

Barrett, P. *Too Busy to Clean?* Pownal, Vermont: Storey Publishing, 1990.

Berthold-Bond, A. *Clean and Green.* Woodstock, New York: Ceres Press, 1994.

Burch, M. A. *Simplicity.* Philadelphia: New Society Publishers, 1995.

Logan, K. *Clean House, Clean Planet.* New York: Simon & Schuster, 1997.

Maine, S. *The Soap Book: Simple Herbal Recipes.* Loveland, Colorado: Interweave Press, 1995.

Schofield, D. *Confessions of an Organized Homemaker.* Cincinnati: Better Way Books, 1994.

INDEX

HERBAL HOMEKEEPING

Sandy Maine

A clean, serene, fresh-scented home—without endless toil OR toxic chemicals? It can be yours with Sandy Maine's easy, all-natural household concoctions. *Herbal Homekeeping* brings cleaning down to earth with thirty safe, economical, and effective recipes, using everyday ingredients and calming, healing, disinfecting essential oils. Maine, author of *The Soap Book* and *Soothing Soaps for Healthy Skin,* turns her expertise to every surface in your home, from kitchen floors and bathrooms to pets, gardens, and laundry. You may never have to buy cleanser again!

INCLUDES INSTRUCTIONS FOR MAKING:

◆ Clever, thrifty Russian Dishwashing Disk

◆ Protective Beeswax Boot and Saddle Conditioner

◆ Ready-in-a-jiffy Once-a-Year Laundry Concentrate

◆ Amazingly effective Tangerine Dream Spot Remover

◆ Soothing, smoothing Healing Shampoo for Dogs and Ca

plus many other formulas for a naturally healthy home

ISBN 1-883010-55-1

51295>

9 781883 010553

$12.95 U.S.
$19.95 Canadian

INTERWEAVE PRESS

P9-DKG-982